Toil the Dark Harvest

Bradshaw Books
Tigh Filí
Thompson House
MacCurtain Street
Cork, Ireland
Phone 353 21 450 9274
Fax 353 21 455 1617
E-mail bradshawbooks@cwpc.ie
Website www.tighfili.com

British Library Cataloguing in Publication Data
ISBN 0 949010 93 6

Cover art *Metanoia 5*, oil on canvas by Joan Hogan
Cover photo by Maeve Edwards
Cover design, typesetting and layout by Nick Sanquest

Printed and bound by Lee Press, Cork.

ceart agus cóir

Grant Aided by
Cork Corporation
Bardas Chorcaí

CORK CITY ENTERPRISE BOARD

the arts council
an chomhairle ealaíon

Toil the Dark Harvest

Geraldine Mills

bradshaw books
Cork, Ireland

Acknowledgements

Thanks are due to the editors of the following in which versions of these poems first appeared:

Poetry Ireland Review, The SHop, Cork Literary Review,
Connemara Life, Western People Awards,
Premio di Poesia Multientnica Città di Olbia, Crannóg,
SIPTU Conference Report, nthposition.com,
Poetry On The Wall, Hometown, Flying Colours.

My gratitude to Máire Bradshaw and the team at Tigh Filí, to Nuala Ní Chonchúir, Vincent Woods, Galway County Council for their Publication Assistance Award and their bursary to the Tyrone Guthrie Centre where this collection was completed.

Special thanks to all at Talking Stick where most of these poems got their first outing.

Contents

For

Tony, Anne, Bernadette, John, Lillian, Tina
Remembering Madeleine

Out of earth's raging
The sea opens like a song
Gilded bowl of sound

Blighted

Your name came to you seaward
upon a ship returning home from Boston
where your mother never settled.
All those brownstone houses starving out the sky,
streets paved with streets, no gold
of whin, or corn at saving, celandine.
Against the tide she bought a passage
on a ship still marked with famine, typhus
back to places that she hungered for,
kept hidden in her shawl your dead sister
until they docked in Cobh and buried her.

Before the year was out
her name was put to use again.
You carried the weight of that ship on your back,
the cold backwash of her eyes,
the way the streets of Holyhoke
seeped into your tight mouth
the sea streeled out from your hair.
You heard the cry of her along the lazy beds
as you barrowed swill to the pigs
caught her on the wing of salt air, your body listing.

Kept hidden in your shawl
a woman longing
to fall upon the wither of that name,
each letter blighted one by one
the sea to open up and swallow them,
to stand at its edge and howl.

Masks

Disturbed by the rain, the woman clears
her table of all domestic things,
turns clay into nose, chin and forehead
gouges out sockets where the eyes should be.

They look out blind from the earth in her hands
as she listens to the hum of her washing machine
familiar and safe taking out the grime
of her home, her children, her working man.

Brown earth faces line the shelves of her dresser,
she lets them dry jaw to jaw on the draining board,
in the deep window-ledges like scones cooling,
the colour of Mayan gold, on the mantlepiece.

She tears up the floor boards and buries them
with beans, amaranth and cotton.
They stare back at her through the cracks in the timbers
as she steps from stove to table with fresh coffee
or turns to draw the curtains on the night.

What We Understood

It was enough for her to say *smell that*,
the hazel that one of us was sent to pick
brandished before us, threatening
as she lined us up against the kitchen wall,
moving the stick under nose after nose *smell that.*

All summer our teeth sank into its unripe nut
not given time to harden against us,
we dug our nails in and under the hazel embryo,
scooped it out, ate it like crumbs of shop bread
white and soft. Hadn't she told us every year,
hives we'd be full of them, glutting on kernels still raw,
scratching all night till she was worn out
painting us with calamine.

That morning when she told me to run
to the neighbours with the message and not forget,
I ran past the tinkers' camp in the hazel trees,
their dog's breath curling white in the cold air;
past the haunted house, the clear of the spring well,
repeating over and over again,
tell Mrs Topping your father's dead
remember tell her.

Your Poem

Those secret days, those nights your body
spooned to mine like wild honey made me beautiful.

Even in your sleep you rhymed my eyes,
my thighs, my hair that strayed across your face;
that I believed I was your queen and you my falconer.

Here in this stolen bed the sky tossed with tercel feathers,
you held my face as if it were your precious bird come home

till your wise mouth tasted salt, and you went back
with stardust in your eyes, for all to see
though never guess, it was I who was your lure.

I was your poem when all the lines were mine, the lyric
of your body mine, the stanza missing in between. The hidden.

Iphigenia

There is no myth in how the storm squalls round the house
or how the gods are out for blood but
something will change the mind of winds tonight.

They howl like demons at the windows of my room
while the boats wait restless in the bay, and I know
as sure as rain beats off the grass that he will come.

He will stand beside my bed and say there is no other way
that I have known the way he looks at me
with no father's eye, while I pass the bread to him

so that my mother will not guess or if she does, holds nothing
of how he will use my sweet breasts, my limbs to be lifted high
by the elders, gag my mouth with a cord, heedless of my cries.

There is no myth in the knife sharp as daffodils
that spear the frozen earth that he will hold to my neck
where a lover might kiss the part of neck
that lovers kiss, my hair pulled back.

He will say it is the thing that fathers do to daughters
so that he can quell the sea, watch his fleet set sail
then put money in an envelope to appease the guilt within.

But how I long to smell the frost rise from the grass
or hold my child that will never be,
(not become a name that dies for Troy)
to watch her pull down apples from a tree.

Pipestrelles

We built our house in the birds' flight path.
Day after day we woke to find
birds dead on the gravel,
an imprint of feather still left on the glass.

But the bats forgave us
and came to an opening
within the cladding of our walls;
hanging weightless until they emerged
excited by twilight slipping from the sky
and we watched the first swoop of them.

They drew us out of ourselves
to watch them flit and feast,
wing parabolas through the air
and squeak into the thin edge of night.

One day while painting the eaves
I found a perfect skeleton,
porcelain bones, wings closed like a locket,
its simian face no bigger than my thumb nail
pressed to the fascia board. Quizzical.

Measuring Niagara with a Teaspoon

After Cornelia Parker, Laing Gallery

In an effort to make sense of it
she has melted then stretched
finely and more finely still,
the silver of a Georgian teaspoon

until its glistening element stretches
the whole fall of Niagara,
all fifty four metres of it.

She has looped and curled,
trapped it in a frame
without the scent of Earl Grey or Darjeeling
to hang on a gallery wall.

Not the way we first saw it,
leaving Cape Cod late
driving all night from state to state
town to storage rentals on the edge of town,

the lonely neons of no vacancies, singing
to keep us from falling asleep at the wheel
while children fractious,
pulled at their seat belts to be free.

Until we arrived bleary-eyed
on the American side as dawn broke,
before bus loads came thundering in.

Its madness came at us like a wild thing,
spat out spray that was struck by the first sun
and moved like lightning through our bodies.
It roared us awake with its foaming electrifying self.

On Seeing Millet's *The End of the Hamlet at Gruchy*

This could be Connemara
and I the mother wearing the red blouse.
I have just run out of my cottage
to see my daughter stand upon the cliff,
put her arms around the elm tree
and try to shake it.
I have abandoned my spinning,
the bread rising in the basin on the table,
the cat sleeping by the fire.
As I reach out to catch her turquoise pinafore
red feathers of boats float on the sea.

I hold onto her while leaves swirl like a tornado
and hens scratch the dirt outside the hen house.
She is all I have in the day
my husband and son gone fishing.
She hums to herself, calls the leaves by their names,
her soft fingers squeezing mine.
I hold her more tightly still for fear the wind
will take her away from me across the water,
to another place, another life,
and I will be left without her smile,
her blonde hair, the eyes of her grandmother.
She does not tire of keeping time with the sky,
of the leaves soughing in the breeze,
but I know by the way the gulls fly
that the wind is changing.

Taking the Heat

Lichened and brittle as spent bones,
they caught the scent of them snapping
as they fell into the trap of their bags –

the sticks she sent them to gather
when there was nothing in the house to burn
but an old shoe or last week's cinders,
picked over for another burning.

And always before they turned for home
they gathered purses of dry moss,
arched the broken sticks to kindle
from a twist of grass to a stolen match.

An old mattress, its horse-hair pulled out
like the centre of loaf bread was piled on top
until it smoked them coughing,
then caught and shot to the blue of the sky.

They took off their clothes
hid them in the camouflage of trees
and young braves that they were
whooped, hollered around the flames.

If she only knew she would have reddened
those pale backsides that were already turning pink
as they dared to see who could take the heat,
hear her call across the trees.

Intruder

The night the heat drove you to take
your bed out onto the balcony,
when the wind came in off the sea
roughing the leaves of the tamarinds,
I didn't follow.

Separate we slept with nothing to soften
the insistence of cars on the street,
and separate I woke to the sound
of the sun coming up over the lagoon.

A sparrow had come in the night
and settled as close as possible,
in the crumple of sheet beside you
as if she couldn't bear to be without you.

I watched you both
the pulse in your neck now easy,
your arm nesting her
head tucked into her breast, plump with sleep.

Sensing my breath in the air
she opened her wings and flew from you,
leaving behind some soft imagining of her self
curved and pale.

Naming of Him

My mother is giving away her past. To one of us
a china cup and to one her thimbles, to another
again a woven afghan she once had stitched with surety.
She is putting in order before she goes old letters, receipts,
rent books, references for work when work was in it.
There is nothing here of her London days:
a door closed on sirens, windows sandbagged,
her new years of married life,
or how she took the mail boat with her first sons
to a house safe in the west of Ireland.
She returned just once
a decade or so after this photo was taken
which she hasn't shown us till now,
one touched by the shadow of winter.

This is my past though I am not in it,
Bundoran nineteen fifty, out of season, but enough work
across the border to keep my parents settled.
They go into Sligo for the day, have tea in a café,
he buys her a coat, she feels beautiful.
They come back laughing with a camera,
the only one in the village, take photographs
of the ducks flattening spring cabbage,
locals with bundles of sticks on their backs, their children.

They stand with a backdrop of willow,
my elder sisters and brothers
age two to twelve, all eyes cast down, except Jimmy.
He looks, holding his dog Pedro
straight at the lens of the new camera,
as if he can tell beyond this day of promise,
full of sweet cake and apples from Sligo town;
to another year in a London street,
the car he doesn't hear, its impact.

At eighteen I went in search of him,
London in the seventies
my first summer job on Half Moon Street.
All I knew was the call that came to the priest's house
while my mother was in town that day
and how he told her coming out of a shop
laden down with Christmas buying.
The mail-boat journey back alone to bury him.
I took the tube to Harlesden station
and found the cemetery from receipts
that came year after year for its upkeep;
then walked line after line of marble names
found nothing of where he entered and too quickly left.

Visiting Cullercoats

They painted the women dragging the lifeboat along this stretch,
their arms strong as rope from gutting fish
and pulling it into the sea to rescue the crew of the Lovely Nellie.

Now a man walks out of it.
The smell of chip butties and mushy peas
comes right down onto the beach where we sit
huddled, looking out towards Tynemouth, South Shields
and at his skin, raw from the beat of the North Sea
the cold February sky.

As his feet touch sand, I notice his footprints
at odds with one another,
not like the trail left by gull or dog,
the primeval step of Adidas.

He walks up onto the strand
past children throwing rain at a wave
and removes his left leg, doll pink, bloodless,
stands and dries it,
leans it against the lifeboat – beached.

Resentment

Raw – it smells
like nothing ever smelled
of Eve's seduction,
of Herod's fateful loss.

It puts out shoots
on long
and sunless days
not knowing
what was said
to make it ripen –

then ripens more,
fruits,
bursts upon
the unsuspecting.

Casting Off

That November he started leaving it all behind:
bonfires, hideouts, his body streaked with charcoal,
spearing the grass, boy hunter,
or in flippers, snorkel, deep-sea diving
the unfathomed territory of the kitchen floor,
two coke bottles tied together the air tank
the shark in him swimming away.

To hold him back, I spent the day
collecting firewood, kindling.
He stood by, no coat,
shoulders hunched in the frost shivering
while I worked to try and get it going.
The fire smoked, flamed for a little while,
he went back to the house.

Maybe that's why I brought him hawking,
to a school of kestrels, peregrines, tawny eagles
a harrier hawk called Wexford.
The falconer showed him how to fasten
the bird upon the leather gauntlet,
lace through the rungs in its claws,
then round his own fingers. Tightly.
He learned its need for raw flesh
how it flew from tree to tree
wind hover
without sound,
swoop
to whip the morsel from his outstretched fist.

Then my turn, the gauntlet on my hand
the bird upon it, me nothing more than a branch.
We walked through the woods my arm raised,
elbow by my side till we came to a clearing
mellow with beech leaves.
The bird, its yellow beak, its autumn wings, waited.
I stretched out my hand
and moving it up and out, cast off.

Burning Earth

I went to see volcanoes crouching, below
a quarter moon that beamed and reddened

and later a moth with only lightness,
quivered above the sullen craters.

I went to smell their spice-hot odour:
habanero chillies, poblano, cayenne

the seethe of rage below the surface
knew that they would spark if threatened.

Boiling phlegm, black sand like poppy seeds,
spilled along the bowl of beaches,

except for palm trees that raked and bowed
against the quiet of high skies,

pretending nothing happened.

Return

After the violence of his going
the trees returned.
They waited for his footfall
but no footfall came.
The days searched out for themselves
while seedlings that once lay
dormant to his step
found earth and air and light,
shot open to the world.

Soon alder, hazel and mountain ash
sprang up where his path should be;
stretched above the window-ledge
to spy through broken panes
and see his mug still on the table,
the Child of Prague headless,
his bike leaning against the stairs,
while a wing of curtain fluttered
against the glass, with no hand
to pull it back and set it free.

Stretcher Board

The chance of it happening again –
you and me meeting on the street like that
both rushing to different ends,
you drinking coffee as you went.

Your shopping list could have been
your martingale, holding your head down
as you hurried for green paint and butter
and tablets for the horse.

You had fifteen minutes
which we filled with talk of Vettriano,
how he never got to art college either
and look at how well he got on.

We checked out old postcards in the antique shop
Andalucia nineteen-o-five, washerwomen
wringing their dirty linen in the sun. Loggers
from Vancouver lumbering pine into carts –

till memory gripped us by the cuff,
your sons and mine trekking across the mountain
never to be so beautifully young again,
the sun a halo round their hair and shining

on the remnant of canoe above your kitchen door
frog and sea creatures (indian red) carved in high relief,
that your grandfather brought back from the Haida,
a stretcher board you said, made to keep two sides apart.

Letters from the Holy Land

i.m. JH: died and buried in Haifa 1935

Wedged, like a shard of glass between Egypt and Jordan
the Holy Land hung from the classroom wall
and the black seeds of Haifa, Acre, Tel Aviv
planted along its ridge meant nothing to me
until my mother showed me letters from her brother
while he was stationed there,
name places he first learned behind seminary walls,
a place he left too soon, never to make them proud,
bestow on them his first blessing
and for shame could never show his face again.

I shall,
        begin from the night I left you
though I am too full of words, Mount
Olivet in front of my window, so barren
I wonder if Christ ascended from it
yet the trace of his right foot is there.

The 'Orontes'
        sailed out from Tilbury and
I wished I could go back, not onwards to
the Bay of Biscay, Naples. We left the ship
at Port Said, and took the train to Scopus.
There I was given two suits of khaki,
two pairs of boots, some stockings,
my civvies shirt sent home. They set me up
with a Lee-Enfield, a hundred rounds
and handcuffs to lock my rifle to my bed.
Your photo got crumpled in my pocket
while we were out on manoeuvres.

I went down
        to the Wailing Wall last night
it was dark, deserted and searching I found a note
beautiful and black and though not knowing
what it said, what sounds it made, its vowel points
it had the look of prayer about it and if I could
I would have sung it there and then but for
bells ringing, shots being fired in the distance.
You know I miss 'The People' and the 'Evening Herald'.

My beat
        from night to dawn is the Street of Prophets,
Mount Calvary, the Stations of the Cross, Gethsemane,
names I practised once, let fall from my tongue
like locust bean. Now I walk them, streets so narrow
I can touch both sides with outstretched hands,
at times hear the sound of the veil being rent in two,
the cock crowing. I go back and switch on my radio
to a chorus of Broadway Melody and Laugh Clown Laugh
and we all as happy as the day is long. Tomorrow
I take two prisoners to Acre for execution.

All roads
        lead to Jerusalem – today the Passover,
yesterday Nebi Mousa, tomorrow Easter.
For two shillings a day I guard the Last Supper room
while down by the wall Jews wail, the Arabs beat
their drums on the other side, and I dream of curlews
calling among the market sounds of Hebrew,
bog myrtle hidden among heather as the wind
murmurs between the olives.

But down
        Gaza way is the worst
and if ever I wanted to go home it's now
night duty chasing bandits, contraband
and the sand, nothing but sand down towards Sinai
the Egyptian Frontier when all I long for
is the taste of rain on my face, the soft of peat underfoot.
I saw the cock-eyed world in Tel Aviv
but had to leave before the end,
another clash in Ekron. You could go back
to Moses and find no different. The Jewels
and the Judges spread their ghostly influence
and from every stone and mound rise the spirits of the past
marching in procession down the valley of Jesophat
where all will be assembled on the last day
no matter who we are. I should have written
sooner but didn't have a stamp.

Call Notes

First the crackle, was the way she remembered,
then the squawk and skirl of the tuning in,
wired to the one and only socket
in the bruised street end house, till
his voice filled the kitchen and his name
(all one word in her mind)
took her into a world out of doors.

There she heard
the *svi svi* small talk of wren
the robin with its hundred phrases
singing just to recognise itself,
never the same song twice.

Brought her out into that time just before dawn
when the wind drops and sounds travel;
(the threats, the slaps, the crash against the floor)
air clear to carry the dawn chorus, tuning in to
the *trru, trru-trru* of thrush,
who sang each song twice over.

Brought her to places beyond
plates breaking, bottles spaced
like swallows on the wires,
waiting for the off.

Memory of Water

This solitary experience.
Maybe it comes
from a moment in the womb –
feeling of saturation, of amnion,
or a past life where I was hooded,
arms tied to my side, thrown into the river,
to test if I would float or die. Die anyway.

Once standing on the edge of it,
its mercury licked the hairs on my legs,
stroked my ankles with its lure
its name foaming darkly;

I gave way, slipped in, my lungs filled up,
hair streamed out like snakelocks
my body folded over.

Out of Old Stories

The Shadow and the Heart

These days the skies hurt with blue,
the flames of earth are lifted and carried
across the stone terraces that reminded you
of fields around Leam, Recess, Gortacarnaun.
We have never know such heat, the locals say
and look how the snails sit tightly packed
as corncobs on the tops of fence posts.

The mulberries have injured us with their juice
like the last time we picked them together;
it bled the length of our arms, down legs,
mixed with the sweat of our bellies.

When out of nowhere but somewhere the rain came
we trapped it in the waiting bowls of our hands
and you told me that if a shower of rain came
while the sun shone, a fox's wedding was taking place.

Touching my face you turned me to where you said
you saw them coming through the olive trees,
the vixen's blazing tail covered in Queen Anne's lace,
her cheeks rouged with mulberry,
a canny look in the groom's eye

and you slipped away, followed the bridal party
out along the lemon trees, through the chicken run,
strewing them with caper flowers.
Out along the camino, a wilderness of dust,
slipped with them down the mountainside
your basket of fruit spilled on the ground.

The Painstaking

The clothes conceal the skin
the skin the bone
the bone the marrow that holds the cry
for fear it might be heard.
No one hears the sound the marrow makes.

She reads that in Potalovo
they strew their graves with antlers,
everything is upended and split open;
enamel pots and kettles, toys dismembered,
offerings to the dead damaged on purpose;
for everything broken in this world
is whole in the next.

The surety of this,
her sweeping brush upon the floor
gathering crumbs, sloughed skin, dog hairs;
her son sitting where the door opens
sunken cheeks, scarred arms, half in
half out.

In a Far-off Mayfly Season

Diggers hulk upon our road on their way
to pile drive another foundation into bog.
Our house shudders and all pictures tilt.

Persimmons fall out of bowls,
wine flows back into jugs, a cat into a gramophone.
Footballs caught in triumph slip out of grasp;
the sleeping maid whose pots and pans slide
into the next room beyond the frame
sink below the rising water table.

In a far-off mayfly season a fisherman
will catch his hook in our window frame
and reel in the cleaned bones of it;
he will place it in his boat beside two trout
his box of bait, not knowing

how a man and a woman
their two children, look out at trees
that crouch like a lioness,
a fox blazing against snow,
or where they lay their heads at night
she in the curve of his sleep
he closer to the door to protect her.

The Potter s Field

Too bloodied to be returned to the temple, the high priests
took the silver, the price of him on whom a price was set
and as a burial place for strangers bought the potter's field.

Thirty pieces were as good to him as a year's work
of cracked amphorae and terracotta bowls
as he looked out over the valley of Hinnom.

Little more than scrub, nothing grew from its red clay
and the one living tree the goats had stripped
of its glaucous, notched leaves.

With the money burning in his pocket
and graves mapped out for strangers
the potter closed his shop, took to making statues.

From the scorched clay of the valley he smoothed
and shaped limb by limb until the body of a woman formed.
When he went to carve her eyes they filled so full of heartbreak

his hands shook. At night when he turned to his wife
they haunted him and he climbed from his bed
to shape them into something more of promise,

but they blazed with the memory of the angel, a shimmer
of gold on his stockings, gems on his shoes, the quiet settling
of his gilded wings as he stood his ground by her chair.

The potter toiled, to change them to a day full
of future, not of neighbours walking
the three steps of compassion with her,

men holding their hats over their breastbone
while her son passed with his cross and looked out over
the Hebron before giving up, the robber free on a technicality.

He shivered as the sky of her eye darkened
and in that time cities, forests, bombs fell,
mothers' milk polluted.

His wife could not bear to watch him dawn after dawn
his face raw from lack of sleep turn in his bed, get up again,
all the wine in the world not helping to forget.

He started to ramble up into the mountains,
look down upon the field he had betrayed.
The world turned to clay in his mouth.

Crafting

1. Graphic Artist

As far back as I can remember
my father carved my path so I would marry,
if not him
then someone so much like him,
he crushed my dream of pen or brush.

It took his death and a failed marriage
for me to draw insects' wings broken;
birds, their bodies stiff with brown claw,
white underbelly exposed.

I drew from the insect's failed wing
when I too was full of half shape and form,
wing and body of it, until the grief
of my own word began to fade.

2. Sculptor

When word began to fade
I turned to stone,

to search out my own language
in round forms of granite,

hands big as the slabs that bezelled
my words on black kilkenny stone.

From earth's hardness I wrote
'there is stone or nothing'.

3. Calligrapher

Nothing is the inside of the quill,
my teacher warned
when she saw me write
in a hand turned to the sweep
and hairline tail of it.
From nothing I paint
the saint's rock gold,
the serif of Bolus Head,
scroll the ancient cruciform
carved into rock,
make legible the monks' calling,
the fulmar's glide

4. Writer

and somewhere a fulmar gliding,
with air its lightness,
shadows its wing in a triangle of room.
A scrap of window opens out
onto the sky and the wintering of things.

The table at which I write is carved
with the burrow of woodworm,
whose tracery of destruction
reads like calligrapher's script
among splashes of artists here before me.

The smell of poison that rises
from the pockmarks at my writing arm,
is that same smell
of which my childhood reeked.

How my mother waged war
against them all her life,
gave us the order to point the canister gun
into the doorways of their homes
one by one. This was no Passover.

We picked out their stiff bodies
with the darning needle,
before legs buckled on chairs;
beds on the beach of lino,
wardrobes crashed,
a dust fine as gold
panned upon the floor.

5. Nomad Artist

When I broke through the pantry window
of the Big House longing for stories
told in the gather of a fire,
I found their lives strewn upon the floor.
Boards curved like waves
with photographs, newspapers
a telegram to say they had arrived.

There were letters torn in two, rolled,
layered like honeycomb
into the square of a biscuit tin,
sent from daughter to mother.
Half histories of names that filled her sleeping;
afternoons of camomile lawns, the opera

and I wondered night after night
what it would be like to have a mother
to write to as I wandered from place to place
to seek my unwritten life
in the skimped faces that are forever
trying to get out from behind
the shadow of oil and ink and gesso.

About Lifelines

Aunt Una had difficulty with ageing.
She watched hands, counted
the creeping of liverspots
the wrinkle of skin, its weathering.
Hands were a dead give-away as were necks
she was heard to say, and measured
a person's years by the way skin lived.

Aunt Una drank white wine
as if it were part of her past,
the silver boa that girdled her wrist
eyed me with its ruby glint,
her nails gaudy and false.

'So easy to forget', my mother sniffed,
coats thrown on the bed for warmth,
frogs that hopped in under the door in the wet
and landed in the tin basin with the bread.

Aunt Una would hold my hand up against hers,
measure its import, its mortality and say
"see what the years will do to you"
flicking the snake of ash from her ivory holder
into my father's cap.

I didn't like her talking like that,
my hands were my own business,
and anyway she was old,
old and scrawny as the chicken
my mother plucked in the back kitchen,
her hair covered in a pink head scarf,
the smell of singeing feathers about to choke the air.

Pearl

The grit that found
its way in under your nail
turned the finger septic,

you a young girl sent over
on the boat with your brothers
to toil the dark harvest,

pickers bent over like question marks,
knuckles skinned,
trawling the ridges for tubers

only fit for sleep
after bowls of what
you'd picked, boiled,

sleeping on straw in the women's bothy
to dream of gloves
with jewel buttons, necklaces.

What happened after that
is gone with you
except that the nail abscessed,

the bed of it infected;
no oyster way to mantle it layer over layer
of nacre, reverse its taint to lustre, pearl,

instead lanced and lanced again
it lost its memory
to grow straight

but ridged and beaked like abalone
grew a further eighty years
among the perfect others of your right hand

and funny how laying you out,
the undertaker painted it
mother-of-pearl, lustrous, absorbing light.

Cutaway Philosophers

Turfed out of Dublin for the summer
we came running to our grandfather
and the bogs of Galway; townies
un-learned in the way of how a sleán
in the hands of the wise slices into mystery.

What they talked of while he footed,
clamped the wet sods with his neighbour
we took no notice; dull as the monotony
that they shaped while we shook
birds from their hiding places,
scratched the shine from our shoes
in the squelch of bog bitter.

Fired by other elements, we never asked
how the wind curled round the asphodel
or the world spun in the cutting into history;
how time put a skin on axe-heads, bog butter, bones
or how it was that given earth, air and water
we would be bringing home fire.

Singing the Dark

I am a woman sitting in the woods at midnight
by a fire on an upturned blue bucket.
I search the darkness for what I can see;
an outline of trunk, of branch
a silhouette of fern curling,

but I pick up wood tunes
as flames play the dried kindling,
the plainsong of leaf in the breeze,
the round of the river way off.

My cat pads down through the trees,
his whiteness picked out by the flame,
makes his way onto my lap, settles.
For one moment there is complete quiet,
the fire is silence glowing red;
I stare into the heart of it.

The cat purrs: I stand and follow
the path towards the river
– wood smoke in my hair –
until I hear where the lines are hidden
in the crunch of my step on twigs,
on the needle-sharp of holly leaves.

I slip off my shoes, step into the river;
catch the sound where my feet hit
night water for the first time,
wash my face in its dark.

Annaghdown Drowning 1828

...Ach lá chomh breá leis gan gaoth ná báisteach,
Lán a bhháid acu 'scuab ar shiúl...
Antoine Raftaire

My scarf would have saved us that day,
tamped in the wound of wood ribs
where the sheep's foot foundered;
it would have held the lake in its pheasant's eye
if not pulled out; that man's coat stamped in place
with such force, the ribs let out their cry, cracked.
In that frame of sound I saw my basket
with fresh eggs, butter newly salted, sink.
The pheasant's eye that only ever knew the hair
of my head floated off, its jade neck darkened.

I let go of the scarf that kept my head warm
when the winds blew in the gap of the house,
I was a hand waving to the last of sky
above the Corrib, Menlo, Bushy Park,
I let go of a sky that showed me kingfishers;
the echo of gulls on their way to the sea,
let go of the small grasp of my son holding
as the dog licked cracked eggs off my boots.
I let go of the tips of my fingers, the last of me
to breathe air on that September day. Touch
the world on my skin, hairs on my knuckles standing.

Sheep sank, (bubbles of bleating from their mouths)
and like white rocks from some foreign beach
filled the hole waiting in the deep for us.
The man who gave his greatcoat to the gash
so close to the shore, longed for its return,
to cover the skin of his back gone cold;
but the sleeves ballooned, fish swam through
their coral reef in a western island lake,
emerged, were shape of those who drowned before us.
We sank into them, scarfskin turned silver,
from scale into gill. Changed, became fin skin.

Maybe Heaven Rejoices

So he thinks he's clever,
returning home like this,
when we had given him up for lost.

Nothing is too good for this son of mine,
who broke my heart from the day he was born,
suckled till my nipples bled dry;
grew big enough to demand his share
then took off, to swill wine,
grow big in some whore's bed.

He didn't worry about his father
who spent nights under the olive tree,
his eyes so red with weeping he never saw
his first born who stayed behind
to plough the fields,
days he spent fatting the calf
when this scut can come back
be sorry for his spending
knowing his father, soft as he is
will forgive all.

He sits in the shade of the palm
(while his brother turns the calf on the spit)
he plays with the gold on his finger,
his feet cool in his new sandals.

Turner in January

How a box built to hold the dark
so that nothing of the day steals in
opens into January light;

spills out colour beginnings
a man who sold skies,
pencil and wash across the page

dissolved in tinted mist
ships, domes, bridges

so that Great Yarmouth harbour
is barely there, Lake Lucerne
or Hastings

and how as light stretches
it lengthens its own dark.

Saint Kevin Dreams

The bird that has nested in the paten of his hand
all those years is ready for change.

Out of wing comes arm, legs grow long and shapely,
its beak softens to that of a woman's lips.

She takes his hand gnarled from years of holding out
moulds it to the sway of her hips

as she leans her cheek against the raspness of his beard
and the scent of distant bellbirds come to him.

He hears music in corners, a bandoneon
its bittersweet counterpoint,

and Kevin is dancing out across the floor
knowing she must follow.

The tanguero sings *Milonga Sentimental*
the air is taut as knife blades.

One two three he leads, his hand to the small of her back
four five six, her dress tight, her heels rise and fall

and his leather sandals that only ever knew
earth and penance now glimpse sky, soaring.

Riverbed

There was an arm's length of bed between them
and no way of telling how that came to be,
or why this august day when he awoke
his hand reached out to touch the familiar
of her skin and rising they drove
across blankets of bog, a cluster of arable
till they came to a river with a rock
that jutted like a peninsula
into its centre just beyond the bridge.

Within the shelter of its bank,
of bog and dobey stuff and shale,
they lay their sleeping bags on the flat bed of rock,
smoothed by its element to pillow their heads
and the yield of their bodies.
He covered her eyes from the glare of the sun
and they slept to the deep river voice,
warm and remembering, like some singer
from a radio piece long ago, turned down low,

while the noon sun arched over them
and a hiker sat on the bridge with his lunch
before he tackled Máiméan
gave them up to their sleep, the water
folding and unfolding around them
like bolts of silk, silver with purple thistle heads.

Boy at the Window Waiting

If he remembers it will be ordinary things:
paint peeling, the old bakelite switch,
her tweed coat the colour of shearwaters,
its sleeve curved to the underwing of her elbow.
It hangs alone in under the stairs where he hid
from her sad eyes and her step that paced the floor
above him, knowing that her body held the muscles to soar.

Walking along the green road to the cliff
where white feathers of foam broke the bread of land,
seabirds gliding she lifted up her arms;
stretched them. There was the whisper of upstroke,
the whole of their flapping that captured the up draught
and let her feet leave. Away up over the Atlantic;
past scree sliding down the hill, rabbit holes,
walls built in defence of wind until there was only sky.

She cried 'I the mother of Icarus brought up in this land
of mean sun, will fly.' Letting go of everyday myth
steamed up in a pot of potatoes, bread sliced like waves;
wallpaper coming down, a coat frayed at the cuffs.

Art at the House of Manrique

It is where the cat comes down to drink,
to this edge of pool,
cool and underground
shaped from the curve of a lava bubble.
She has come from
the blistering heat above earth,
to crouch at its rim,
touch the water with her tongue.

Down the lava steps
she wanders from bubble to bubble,
pays no heed to the gecko
on the glistening white of floor.
Then up again past the triptych of bones
into the upper level art rooms where
she sits by one of the windows,
washes herself.

A visitor, come to feast on big names
turns his eyes from the cubes and lines
in front of him to watch
her sinuous body rise, stretch.
She goes from room to room
from Miró to Picasso,
nonchalant in their presence.

She slinks by the legs of tourists
takes the slow deliberate walk
across the tiles
and everyone turns to watch
a black cat with a white collar
walk across a cool marble floor.

Flock Memory

He lost the way of working with his days;
no white stones of sheep to count at night,
no anxious dawn to pull a sickly lamb,
the prize ram culled, the raddle on its back
wiped out when Herod's lackeys came.

A new flock wouldn't know to move from field to field,
track the scent of grass through the gap in the wall
nor find the stonefort on the hill to shelter from bad days
where Ann Farrell and her baby lay.

In spring the hawthorn won't draw them close,
as magpies sit and watch white petals fall
like bones into a flame; a notice on his gate,
a snag of wool on wire.

Poet as Magpie

She flies in on the sniff of a line
to thieve it from the gaping mouth
of the storyteller – hard lived –

then sits in the trees, grackles,
pecking at it piecemeal
wondering how to put fat on it.

Adds to it a grain of untruth
that she steals from the cat's bowl,
nothing is black and white after all.

She pretends it's hers to swallow
the lore of the fox or a mother's venial past,
one for sorrow, six for gold.

She brings each pilfered piece back to her store,
sits on it while the farmer turns his gun on her,
then spits it back at him – a secret not to be told.

Astrolabe

This was the way Hypatia taught me;
to cut and shape the flat disc first,
calibrate its scale around the edge
get its arm to pivot and by degrees
I'd learn the time of day.

Each life's hour I worked on it
blind to darkness emptying outside,
attached two eyeholes matching up the sights
till day came spilling in.
I brought it to her, my gift
and what she saw as competence was love.

Though she argued that beauty was illusion
all of Alexandria talked of hers,
the men with longing, the women with their scorn
as they gathered in the marketplace
to count the scales of fish or sniff out spices
as good women do.

They watched to see her white cloak pass
and mock us young men running to her word

and mocked us still when forced to find
the eye within; but the I within me
could only see the sky blue of her own,
the curve of breast beneath her cloak.

To unlearn this weakness in me, make me rise
above the flesh, she rubbed my nose
in her soiled and bloodied underclothes
but the instrument of my body calibrated to my want
just made me want her more

till whispers started seeping from church walls,
her name from mouth to ear like wasp stings.

In darkness when souls turned black
and days of fasting were posted on the door
I came out to focus on some unknown star
and setting up my sights
saw the man with a black shell to his ear
whistle to someone on the lower balcony
as her chariot came down the street

and know it was too late to cry *Hypatia, Hypatia*
my voice lost while Christians oozed from shadows
pulled her from her carriage, their oyster shells
like razors to hack her flesh to pieces.

Nights I stand in the marketplace
watch the sky above me inscribe her chariot,
her cloak white across the firmament.
I take out my astrolabe and with its sharpened arm,
pluck out the eye buried deep within me.

I would have the sky lash me with its stars
the world spin off its axis
never know the time of day.

Fruit Falling

It is the morning of my daughter's leaving.
She is still asleep,
her cases in the hall eager to be gone
while I have packed all I will
into the seed purse of her memory.

She leaves stars on the floor for me to sweep up,
sky fires fallen from some show,
some moment when she shone.

Haws ripen, guelder swells with the future,
apples shiver in the waiting light,
are learning the language of letting go.
She will find her own fruit, pick and eat it,
follow its scent on the wind.
I am a small branch bending.

Throat Singer

The only world she ever knew was the one
she sang and the singing made.

A seal breathing holes in the ice
almond smell of icebergs.

The wind's eye through the hut
the northern light coming near.

The drone of rocks in the river
their overtone in the sky.

As if a Bird

and seeing with its gimlet eye
a hawk maybe or even an eagle
that crossed the sky from Morena
to Montes de Toledo,
let go the slink of small animals hiding
the eye in him so full of shape of land;
the spurge, the clotted fields and gorges
his shadow – though smaller – with him
his perfect shadow self.

The land fractured below him, collage of fields,
of lines and squares and cubes and he saw
for the first time from above and all around
the parched earth, the colours given
madder, sienna, ochre,
the way the light waned in the Barranco
whatever trees, the dry riverbed a salamander.

For Shame

Long before we ever put a shape on it
we ate its cunning fruit.
Father wore it with his navy blue apron
that he put on every day of his life
or covered with his trilby hat
for the five-mile cycle to the shop.

It had no fear of mothballs
was in the brass ends of the bed,
in the foxing of the dozen books or so
on the window-ledge. It grew fat on us.

Too big to fit under the stairs,
it seeped out onto the black and white tiles,
up onto the landing and in through the wardrobe
with the crib and the box of summer clothes on top.

By day we took it on like a sister who was born slow,
but night swam right back with it
when our hands grew too small in the dark to hold it,
brought us to the edge of ourselves.

Wednesday Women

This is where we women meet,
the third Wednesday of every month,
sitting in our padded chairs
deciding to have tea or coffee,
brought to us on lap trays
painted with blue cornflowers.

Outside the rain pours down
on cars queuing for parking space,
on a world wondering by;
while in here we are sheltered
by sunbursts on the curtains,
a music station playing Arvo Pärt.

We ask each other how we've been
since we last met, how well we look
the colour in our hair
so good so real, a perfect match
you could hardly tell the difference.

They come in their purple masks
to plug us in, search out veins now paper thin
so that these Wednesdays
they have to dig them out like lugworms
and send the pain shooting to the stars.

I could wish for the cloth of heaven
to come down and help me forget
how my hair curled around my ears
softening my face, then watch it fall,
come out in fistfuls
a nest of it on the pillow in the morning

and look in the mirror, staring back at me
no eyebrows, no eyelashes.
What are we now we Wednesday women?
What are we now but one breasted hollowed out
women waiting.

The Tree Forgives the Axe

We wouldn't fail to leaf in this place,
cut willow staked in the ground
puts out green in the new season.

When crossed by wind,
we lean like old men into one another
and when things are good we grow.

We hold in our heartwood our strength to stand,
witness in our ring of life the way
the world was then and now;

how Solomon showed his wisdom,
when Gandhi walked to salt.
Jesus healed. Martin Luther had a dream.

We make good the air from jets
that streak the sky,
while women in blue burkahs
hurry home before curfew.

We watch clouds collude,
let our leaves fall like bodies
from towering oaks.

When chopped and nailed into a cross,
we still forgive the axe.

Your Death

And when
it came
there was
no word
for it.

Like Eskimos
who have
over fifty
for types
of snow

but none
for itself.